# The Thai Cookbook

Sweet, Sour, Salty and Spicy Dishes
Originating from Thailand That Are
Totally Packed with Flavour

BY

*Daniel Humphreys*

# License Notes

No part of this Book can be reproduced in any form or by any means including print, electronic, scanning or photocopying unless prior permission is granted by the author.

All ideas, suggestions and guidelines mentioned here are written for informative purposes. While the author has taken every possible step to ensure accuracy, all readers are advised to follow information at their own risk. The author cannot be held responsible for personal and/or commercial damages in case of misinterpreting and misunderstanding any part of this Book

# Table of Contents

# Introduction

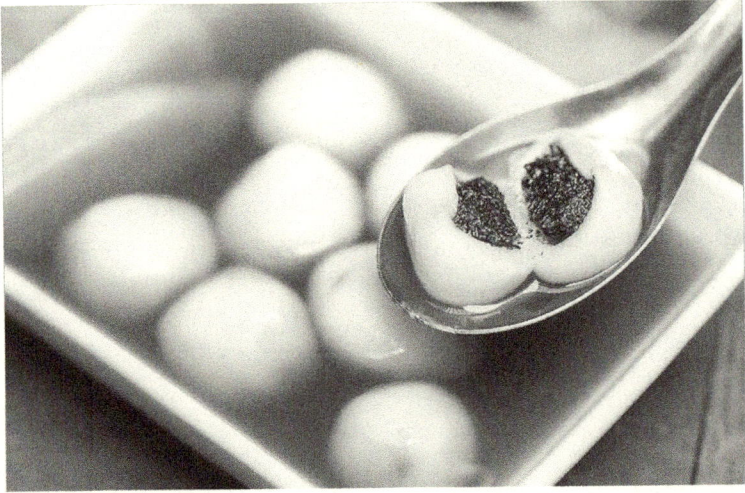

The Thai Cookbook

If anyone thinks that Thai just goes as far as Pad Thai and Massaman curry, then they are sadly mistaken! Those dishes are in this book, because they're deliciously awesome(!), but so are 23 other incredible dishes too, to help you get that sweet, sour, salty and spicy taste that I know you've been craving!

So, it's time to spread your culinary wings and try out Khao Soi (curried noodle soup), Pa Thong Ko (donuts) and Bua Loy Nam Ki (sesame dumplings in ginger soup).

Arm yourself with some ginger, lime juice, fish sauce, sugar and all of the other delicious and fresh ingredients that go into Thai food to give it that perfect flavour and let's do this!

# Tom Yum Goong (Spicy Shrimp Soup)

Let's learn some Thai! 'Tom' is in reference to the fact that this dish is boiled, and 'Yum' (or sometimes 'Yam'), refers to the combination of both spicy and sour. Well, I can confirm that that is exactly what this dish delivers – it does what it says on the tin, if you will. You boil it, and, funnily enough, it tastes both spicy AND sour. But don't just take my word for it, try this recipe out yourself!

**Serves:** 4

**Preparation time:** 60 minutes

**Ingredients:**

- 64 oz. chicken broth
- 16 oz. large shrimp
- 8 oz. mushrooms
- 4 kaffir lime leaves
- 2 limes
- 2 spring onions
- 2 stalks lemongrass
- 2 red chillies
- 2 tablespoons fish sauce
- 1 ½ tablespoons caster sugar
- 1 inch fresh ginger
- 1 stalk fresh cilantro

**Serving suggestion:**

When you need soup but it's summer and so you're feeling something fresh and colourful, then Tom Yum Goong is for you!

1) Pour the chicken broth into a saucepan and bring it to the boil.

2) Chop the lemongrass stalks into 2 inch pieces. Grate the ginger and slice up the red chillies. Add all of these, along with the kaffir lime leaves into the broth.

3) Cover the broth and leave it to simmer for 15 minutes.

4) Meanwhile, peel and chop the mushrooms. Then, when the broth is ready, add them in, along with the sugar and fish sauce.

5) Leave the broth to simmer for 5 minutes, before adding in the shrimp.

6) Then, leave the broth to simmer for another 5-8 minutes, until your shrimp have turned pink.

7) Then, remove from the heat.

8) Chop the spring onions and cilantro, and juice and zest the lime.

9) Stir the spring onion and cilantro in and add lime juice to taste.

10) Taste and adjust the balance of sweet, sour, salty and spicy and garnish with the lime zest to serve.

**Tips:** The lemon grass stalks and kaffir lime leaves are not for eating! You can leave them in the soup to keep the flavour infusing but be sure to remind others (and yourself!) not to eat them!

Aesthetically, nice, big shrimp, with the tails still on look the best, in my opinion. However, having them already peeled is a pretty good idea, to avoid having to make a mess whilst eating!

# Som Tam (Spicy Papaya Salad)

Here's a fast fact for you; in 2011, Som Tam from Thailand was number 46 on a list of the 'World's 50 Most Delicious Foods', compiled by CNN. That alone should be reason enough to give it a try, if you haven't before! This form of papaya may be a little less familiar to many of us, but it's no less worthy! I am a huge fan of papaya in its riper, sweeter, and more orange form! This salad that is, of course, sour, salty, sweet and spicy all in one, as good Thai food should be, uses green papaya, and I've come to appreciate papaya in a whole new way!

**Serves:** 1-2

**Preparation time:** 20 minutes

**Ingredients:**

- 8 cherry tomatoes
- 6 garlic cloves
- 6 chillies
- 3 tablespoons lime juice
- 3 tablespoons peanuts
- 2 tablespoons fish sauce
- 1 green papaya
- 1 cup green beans
- 1 tablespoon sugar

**Serving suggestion:**

This is a lunch with some pizz-azz! Take it to the office and be the envy of all!

1) Peel and de-seed the papaya. Then, grate or shred the papaya flesh.

2) Chop the ends off of the green beans and slice them in half, and then down the middle lengthways too.

3) Chop the chillies, and then crush them along with the cherry tomatoes in a pestle and mortar.

4) Mince the garlic.

5) In a separate bowl, mix together the sugar, lime juice and fish sauce. Stir to dissolve the sugar.

6) Toss all of your ingredients (the crushed chilli mix, minced garlic and the papaya) in the sauce and serve garnish with the roughly chopped peanuts.

**Tips:** Take care when using the pestle and mortar. We are not trying to bash the chillies and tomatoes into a pulp, but simply to crush them slightly to start releasing the juices.

This is supposed to be INCREDIBLY spicy (hence the 6 chillies for 1 serving), but, of course, if your palette isn't yet up to that, you can lower the chilli content.

# Tom Kha Gai (Chicken Coconut Soup)

We have made it to one of my absolute favourite ingredients in Thai cuisine – the coconut! I am absolutely head-over-heels in love with coconuts, and I find that coconut milk specifically is such a delicious base for soups, curries and the like. It's also a great one for those who maybe can't quite handle the spice as the Thai can yet, because coconut cools everything down deliciously, as well as adding a dimension of creaminess that you just can't beat!

**Serves:** 4

**Preparation time:** minutes

**Ingredients:**

- 16 oz. chicken breast
- 14 fl oz. coconut milk
- 14 fl oz. chicken broth
- 1 stalk fresh lemongrass
- 1 inch fresh ginger
- 1 cup mushrooms
- 1 tablespoon lime juice
- 1 tablespoon fish sauce
- 1 teaspoon chilli paste
- ¼ cup fresh cilantro
- ¼ cup fresh basil

**Serving suggestion:**

I know it would be somewhat an infusion of cuisines (but we're not against that, are we?) but serving this with garlic coriander naan bread is fantastic.

1) Slice the lemongrass up and place it into a large pan along with the chicken broth and coconut milk. Bring the mixture to the boil.

2) Meanwhile, slice up the chicken and mushrooms, and then add them into the pan.

3) Stir in the lime juice, fish sauce and chilli paste.

4) Simmer for 5-10 minutes until the chicken has turned opaque.

5) Check that the chicken is done, and then remove the lemongrass.

6) Tear the cilantro and basil and stir them through for just a minute before serving.

**Tips:** To be more on the 'safe side', or to be quicker, you can cook your chicken separately, or use pre-cooked.

As always with Thai food, check the balance of flavours before serving and adjust the levels of sugar, chilli, fish sauce and lime juice to taste.

# Gaeng Daeng (Red Curry)

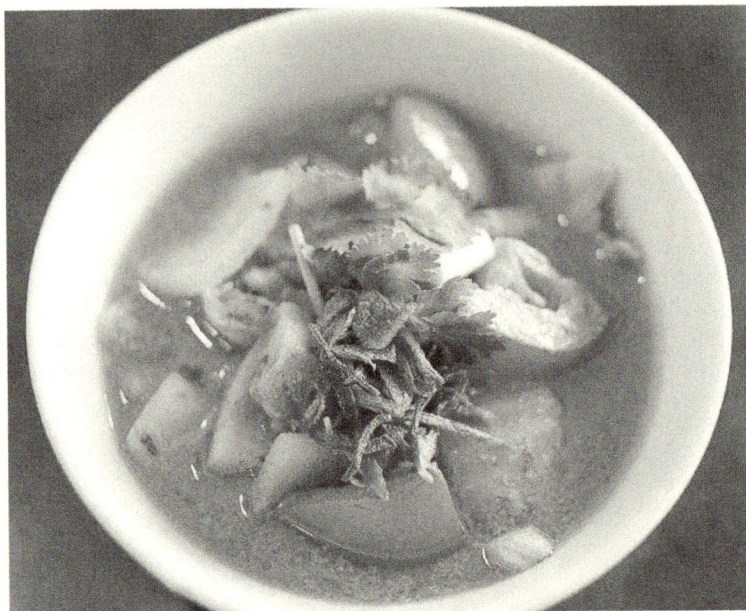

Even if you know nothing else about Thai food, I'm certain you've heard of at least 3 dishes – Thai Red Curry, Thai Yellow Curry and Thai Green Curry. Don't worry, we will be covering them all in this book because each is slightly different to the other and have definitely earned their place in Thai cuisine in their own rights. Essentially, the difference is the peppers used in each of the curries.

Unsurprisingly, red curries use red chillies (which tend to be pretty spicy), green curries use green chillies (which are moderate in spice) and yellow curries use yellow peppers (which are not spicy, although spice still comes from other ingredients). So, get your red chillies ready and let's make Gaeng Daeng, or Thai Red Curry.

**Serves:** 4

**Preparation time:** 35 minutes

**Ingredients:**

**For the curry paste:**

- 10 dried chillies
- 8 red chillies
- 6 coriander roots
- 4 garlic cloves
- 2 shallots
- 2 teaspoons shrimp paste (or fish sauce)
- 2 teaspoons coriander seeds
- 1 stalk of lemongrass
- 1 teaspoon cumin seeds
- 1 teaspoon grated galangal

- ½ teaspoon black peppercorns
- Pinch of salt

**For the curry:**

- 28 fl oz. coconut milk
- 8 chicken thighs (skinless boneless)
- 5 tablespoons red curry paste (recipe above)
- 2 tablespoons fish sauce
- 1 tablespoon vegetable oil
- 1 tablespoon minced ginger
- 1 tablespoon lime juice
- 1 teaspoon brown sugar
- 1 red chilli
- ½ cup fresh basil + extra to garnish

**Serving suggestion:**

Just good old sticky rice, maybe flavoured with jasmine?

1) To make the curry paste; first, set the dried chillies in a bowl of warm water to soak. Then, add the coriander seeds, peppercorns and cumin seeds into a dry pan on medium heat for around 2 minutes until they become fragrant. Then, grind these roasted spices into a powder. Chop the ends off of the dried chillies and red chillies, and finely chop them. Peel and mince the garlic, and finely chop the coriander root, shallots and lemongrass (use the white part only).

2) Add everything into a blender (or a pestle and mortar if you're being traditional) and blend until you have a smooth paste. Add a little water in if you need to, to bring everything together.

3) Heat the vegetable oil in a large saucepan and add in the minced ginger when the oil is heated, so that it begins to sizzle. Then, add in the curry paste and stir.

4) Once the paste has become fragrant, pour in the coconut milk. Bring the mixture to the boil and then reduce to a simmer.

5) Dice up the chicken thighs. Add them into the saucepan and leave it simmering whilst they cook through. This will take 10-15 minutes.

6) Add in the fish sauce and sugar, to taste, and then stir in the basil leaves.

7) Chop the chilli and use it to garnish the bowls, along with more fresh basil leaves.

**Tips:** Store your leftover curry paste in an airtight jar refrigerated for up to a week, or frozen for a month.

As always, the balance of flavours is what makes Thai food. Therefore, don't be afraid to add in the fish sauce and sugar a little at a time and keep tasting it. Remember! - you can add more to taste, but you can't take it out!

# Pad Thai

It has often been said that Pad Thai is the ultimate street food, and I'm pretty close to being convinced of that fact, actually. Bangkok, Thailand is an amazing, bustling city, which really lends itself to quick and cheap food on the go – and competition for it too! That, in fact, is a great thing, because it means that each cart owner has perfected their own recipe, and uses the best ingredients they can, and sells for the best price too! This recipe is kind of a traditional, or 'average' (not in taste, but in normality!) Pad Thai, and boy, are these fried noodles good!

**Serves:** 4

**Preparation time:** 15 minutes

**Ingredients:**

- 8 oz. noodles
- 3 spring onions
- 2 eggs
- 2 tablespoons brown sugar
- 2 tablespoons vegetable oil
- 1 ½ tablespoons fish sauce
- 1 garlic clove
- 1 teaspoon soy sauce
- ½ cup peanuts
- ¼ cup fresh cilantro
- Pinch of red pepper flakes (to preference)

**Serving suggestion:**

This is a whole and perfect dish on its own! If you're looking to bulk it put though, or up the protein content, stir in shrimp or chicken too.

1) Bring a large saucepan of water to the boil and cook the noodles according to the package instructions. It's likely that they'll take between 8 and 10 minutes. Then, drain them and set to one side.

2) Meanwhile, heat the vegetable oil in a large pan and mince in the garlic.

3) Crack the eggs into a bowl and lightly beat them with a fork. Then, add them into the pan and allow them to begin to solidify. Keep stirring and moving the pan around so that you are creating scrambled eggs.

4) Separately, stir together the fish sauce, soy sauce and sugar. Add them into the pan with the scrambled egg.

5) Roughly chop the peanuts and stir them through too.

6) Stir the noodles through the dish, and add in the red pepper flakes, to taste.

7) Tear the fresh cilantro and slice up the spring onions.

8) Serve topped with the fresh cilantro and spring onion and enjoy!

**Tips:** Thai rice noodles are what is used traditionally in Pad Thai, but, unfortunately, these are not always available for a reasonable price. If that's the case, of course you can substitute them for regular noodles, or even a pasta like linguine.

This is a Thai dish that is actually not very spicy! If, like me, you ADORE Thai food but have a family member who's allergic to chilli, then this is the dish for you! You can leave the chilli flakes out and allow everyone to sprinkle them into their dish to their personal preference. The spice of Thai food is great, but the egg and peanuts are the stars of this dish, for me, and the salty sweetness speaks for itself.

# Pad Krapow Moo (Pork Fried Rice)

Yes, I know – a dish with 'moo' in the title should really be made with beef! But, it isn't; this delicious fried rice dish uses pork, as well as a good helping of fresh basil, which is something that I personally just cannot get enough of! So, here's another little lesson in Thai for you; 'Pad' means 'wok fried', 'Krapow' refers to the basil (often called 'holy basil', which I really love!) and the 'Moo' tells us that the protein in this dish is pork. You may see other 'Pad Krapow ...' dishes with different third words, which will be very similar but using a different meat or fish. So, there we go – we're now fluent and can get to cooking!

**Serves:** 4

**Preparation time:** 30 minutes

**Ingredients:**

- 19 oz. filleted pork
- 5 ¼ oz. green beans
- 2 red chillies
- 2 garlic cloves
- 2 tablespoons oyster sauce
- 2 tablespoons peanut oil
- 2 teaspoons brown sugar
- 1 red bell pepper
- 1 cup fresh basil
- 1 teaspoon fish sauce

**Serving suggestion:**

Rice or noodles are really the 2 choices when it comes to Thai!

1) Thinly slice the pork.

2) Put the peanut oil into a pan over a high heat and fry the pork for 2-3 minutes, until it's browned. You may find that it's easier to do in 2 or 3 smaller batches. When it's all done, add all of the pork back into the pan.

3) Add the basil into the pan with the pork, and keep it on a low heat, allowing the basil to heat through and begin to wilt.

4) Stir together the oyster sauce, fish sauce and brown sugar and set aside.

5) De-seed and slice up the red bell pepper and the red chillies and mince the garlic. Add them all into a pan separate from the pork.

6) Trim the green beans and add them into the vegetable pan, along with 1/3 of a cup of water.

7) Stir around in the pan to cook the beans, until the water has evaporated.

8) Add the pork into the veggie pan and stir in the oyster sauce mix. Taste and adjust to your liking, and then enjoy!

**Tips:** If you have it available, you can use buttermilk instead of the lemon juice and milk mix. We decided on that though, as they're more likely to be things you'll have in the house!

This is supposed to be a rustic dessert, to keep your dough dollops random!

# Gaeng Keow Wan Kai (Green Curry)

As one of the most iconic and easy to make Thai dishes, and one that is easy on the palette of those of us not yet accustomed to the spice, Gaeng Keow Wan Kai, or 'Thai Green Curry' is a king amongst curries. It was one of the first dishes that I remember making ever actually, and I feel that it's safe to say that I have got it down to a fine art form. This curry is delicious, and there are always leftovers for lunch the next day, which pleases me!

**Serves:** 6

**Preparation time:** 30 minutes

**Ingredients:**

**For the curry paste:**

- 5 green chillies
- 4 coriander roots
- 2 ¼ oz. galangal
- 2 lemongrass stalks
- 2 garlic cloves
- 2 shallots
- 2 kaffir lime leaves
- ¾ oz. shrimp paste
- ¼ cup fresh basil
- ¼ oz. coriander seeds
- Pinch of cumin seeds
- Pinch of nutmeg

**For the curry:**

- 16 oz. diced chicken
- 14 fl oz. coconut milk
- 8 oz. new potatoes
- 4 teaspoons curry paste (recipe above)
- 3 ½ oz. green beans
- 2 teaspoons fish sauce
- 1 garlic clove
- 1 tablespoon lime juice
- 1 tablespoon vegetable oil
- 1 teaspoon sugar
- ½ cup fresh basil + extra to garnish
- ½ cup peanuts

**Serving suggestion:**

I am not one to shy away from carbs! Yes, this curry has potato in it, but it should be served with sticky rice and naan bread too!

1) To make the curry paste; into a dry pan, put the cumin seeds, coriander seeds and nutmeg. When they have become fragrant, grind them into a powder. Chop and de-seed the chillies and add them into a blender along with the garlic, shallots, coriander roots, galangal and the white part only of the lemongrass. Then, blend in the spice powder, shrimp paste, lime leaves and basil until you have a smooth paste. Of course, to be more traditional, all of this should be done in a pestle and mortar!

2) Set a large pan of water on to come to the boil. Halve the new potatoes and add them in when the water is boiling. Trim the green beans and add them to the pot after 5-7 minutes. After 3 minutes, check that the potatoes are tender but not fully cooked. Strain the pan and set aside.

3) Heat the vegetable oil in a large wok and mince in the garlic. Quickly stir in the curry paste to avoid the garlic burning, and then pour in the coconut milk too.

4) When the coconut oil is bubbling, stir in the fish sauce, lime juice and caster sugar and taste. Adjust the balance of flavours if needed.

5) Roughly chop the peanuts and stir them into the curry, along with the chicken. Cover the wok and leave everything to simmer for 8-10 minutes, to cook the chicken through.

6) Then, stir in the potatoes and green beans, as well as the basil and leave everything to come together for 2-3 minutes before having a final taste check and serving.

**Tips:** Again, with the curry paste, store any leftovers in an airtight jar in the refrigerator or freezer to be able to use it again.

With the flavours in Thai food, especially fish sauce, lime juice and chilli, a little goes a long way. It's always better to add a little less than the recommended amount first and then taste. It's super easy to add in more of something, but flavours cannot easily be removed!

# Yum Nua (Spicy Beef Salad)

Looking for Thai food that's not going to wreak havoc with the waistline? Well, actually, let's be honest, as a cuisine, Thai is amazingly fresh and healthy. Buuuut, it always feels more healthy if we can call a dish a 'salad', am I right? This one is fresh, definitely packs a punch(!), and uses steak – yum! That's a 'yum' in the English sense, as well as the Thai!

**Serves:** 2-4

**Preparation time:** 30 minutes

**Ingredients:**

- 10 oz. strip steak
- 6 romaine lettuce leaves
- 3 cilantro stems
- 2 ½ tablespoons lime juice
- 2 chillies
- 2 tablespoons fish sauce
- 1 ½ teaspoons brown sugar
- 1 garlic clove
- 1 cucumber
- 1 shallot
- 1 lemongrass stalk
- ¼ cup fresh mint leaves
- Pinch of salt
- Pinch of pepper

**Serving suggestion:**

Serve this with a fresh smoothie of papaya and banana to cool you off after the heat!

1) Mince the garlic and de-seed and chop the chillies before blending them together into a paste.

2) Then, thinly chop the white part of the lemongrass and add it into the blender too, along with the lime juice, fish sauce and brown sugar and whiz it all up into a smooth dressing.

3) Add the vegetable oil into a skillet over a medium-high heat. Chop the steak into 1 ½ inch strips and sear in the skillet for 5 minutes on each side.

4) Once the steak has cooled, slice into thinner strips.

5) Dice the shallot and chop the cucumber to your liking (I am totally fine with the skin and seeds, but I know that others aren't!). Roughly chop the cilantro stems and mint leaves and toss everything together with the romaine lettuce to create your salad.

6) Add the steak juices to your dressing.

7) Put the steak strips into your salad, and then pour on the dressing, sparingly at first!

**Tips:** Every pan and steak are different, so do keep an eye on it! Our specified method should give you medium steak, but if you prefer it rarer, or more well-done, then adjust the cooking time to your preferences.

We've made a pretty basic salad base, but go ahead and jazz it up with whatever you like in your salad, such as cherry tomatoes, grated carrot, radishes etc.

# Kai Med Ma Muang (Chicken Cashew Stir Fry)

So, there's a bit of scandal surrounding this dish... it's stolen! This dish most likely made its way to Thailand from China, as something that we probably know pretty well – Kung Pao! Kung Pao is delicious, obviously, and often uses peanuts. Well, the Thai replaced the peanuts with cashews. And, of course, Thai and Chinese are 2 awesome cuisines, so this fusion of the 2 is a food lover's heaven!

**Serves:** 4

**Preparation time:** 25 minutes

**Ingredients:**

- 8 oz. diced chicken
- 2 garlic cloves
- 2 red chillies
- 1 ½ tablespoons soy sauce
- 1 onion
- 1 spring onion
- 1 tablespoon plain flour
- ½ cup cashews (preferably pre-roasted, to save time)
- ½ tablespoon fish sauce
- ½ teaspoon brown sugar
- 1/3 cup dried chillies
- Pinch of ground white pepper
- Oil for frying

**Serving suggestion:**

Noodles are the best accompaniment to stir fry, in my humble opinion.

1) Mix the soy sauce, fish sauce, sugar and a pinch of white pepper with 3 tablespoons of water, and then set aside.

2) Add the cashews into a pan with a little oil on a high heat and toss them until golden.

3) Half the dried chillies and chop off any stems. Fry them too until shiny on the outside.

4) Remove the cashews and chillies from the pan and set on paper towels to absorb any excess oil.

5) Pour the flour onto a dish and roll the chicken in it to coat. 'Deep fry' the chicken (this simply means having enough oil in the pan so that the chicken can be submerged, so with a small dice, you'll probably only need a depth of 2-3 inches). Then, set the chicken on paper towels to soak up the excess oil too.

6) Julienne (thinly slice) the onion and red chillies. Slice the spring onion

7) Wipe the wok clean and add in just a dash of oil. Mince the garlic into the pan and add in the sliced onion.

8) Add in the chicken, cashews and dried chillies and mix everything well.

9) Pour in the sauce you made everything and keep stir frying until it thickens.

10) Stir in the fresh chillies and spring onion for just a minute to keep them fresh still and serve.

**Tips:** If you don't have ready roasted cashews, you can easily do it yourself! Simply spread the cashews out on a baking tray, maybe sprinkle them with a little salt, and roast at 350F for 10-20 minutes, until they have reached the desired colour.

If you're like me and just love nuts, go for even more of a fusion and use a mix of peanuts and cashews.

# Khanom Gluay (Steamed Banana Puddings)

Whilst Thai desserts don't seem to have made such a big impact on Western cuisines as their savoury dishes, that doesn't mean we shouldn't be enjoying them! In fact, if you're not a 'big on desserts' kind of person, then Asian-style desserts may actually be for you! On the whole, these types of desserts tend to be less sweet than their Western counterparts, and actually often very healthy, and free from a lot of the dairy and processed sugars that are often annoying present in desserts.

**Serves:** 8

**Preparation time:** 30 minutes

**Ingredients:**

- 10 bananas
- 3 cups rice flour
- 2 cups sugar
- 1 cup coconut cream
- 1 cup fresh coconut meat
- Desiccated coconut to garnish
- Pinch of salt

**Serving suggestion:**

An easy, light and summer-y dessert for when you need that sweet kick of a summer's evening.

1) Grate the coconut flesh into a bowl and sift in the rice flour.

2) Then, stir in the coconut cream and sugar. Add in a good pinch of salt.

3) Puree the bananas and fold them into the mixture.

4) Pour the mixture into a deep baking tray and then steam in for 20 minutes.

5) Allow the pudding to cool, and then chop into slices and serve garnished with the desiccated coconut.

**Tips:** If you're unsure how to 'steam' the pudding, then let me tell you how! Take a bigger, deeper baking dish and place the dish with the banana pudding it in inside of it. Then, take boiling water and pour it around the edges, so inside the bigger dish so that the water comes up to halfway up the sides of the dish with the banana in it. Then, place it in an oven at 300F and leave it to 'steam'. of course, you may have another preferred method, or a cool gadget, so steam as you like!

In many dishes, riper bananas are better – but not so for this one! In order to get a better texture, just regular ripe bananas tend to work the best.

# Khao Neow Ma Muang (Sweet, Sticky Rice with Mango)

Now, we know that there are 3 main categories of meal – breakfast, lunch and dinner. Society seems to state that after breakfast, really, the other meals should be of the savoury variety, and if you want more sweetness throughout the day, then you either just have all the way until AFTER dinner, or basically, you're a bad person. Well, call me a bad person, but I need some sugar during the day, okay! I may have a found a way around this, though. Rice is most often used in savoury dishes and is almost universally accepted as a healthy and filling lunch choice. So, if I sneakily make my lunchtime rice sweet, then we're all happy, aren't we?

**Serves:** 4

**Preparation time:** 40 minutes

**Ingredients:**

- 2 large, ripe mangoes
- 2 cups white rice
- 2 tablespoons brown sugar
- 1 ¼ cups coconut milk
- Pinch of salt

**Serving suggestion:**

This is all a little bit soft and mushy, to be honest, and so if you're a bit of a texture snob, then you can top this with something crunchy too. The Thai often go for toasted mung beans, for example.

1) Into a saucepan, put the ice, coconut milk, sugar, 1 1.4 cups of water and a good pinch of salt.

2) Bring the pan to the boil and then reduce it down to a simmer, and leave it simmering for 8-10 minutes, until you can see that all if the liquid is absorbed, but that your rice still has that awesome sticky texture to it.

3) Then, remove the pan from the heat and cover it, leaving it to stand for 5 minutes.

4) Meanwhile, you could use this time to peel and slice your mangoes, and then keep them stored in the refrigerator until you need them.

5) Once the rice has sat, it needs steaming for 15-20 minutes. You may already have a steamer that you can use, or you can use the 'double saucepan' method. Here, you will fill a saucepan about halfway up with water and set it to boil.

Then, you will sit your saucepan of rice on top of that pan (so it's helpful if they are a similar size and are stackable).

6) Then, you can divide your rice into the individual portions, egg in ramekins, and let it cool.

7) When ready to serve, tip the rice out of its mould onto a plate and top with the fresh mango and a light sprinkle of salt

**Tips:** Adding some coconut yoghurt and other fresh fruit to this dish will really make it into something special; maybe even a great breakfast idea!

If this is something you will be doing often, then it may be a good idea to invest in a Thai basket for steaming. This is how the Thai have been doing it for centuries, and so we do trust their equipment!

# Khao Mao Tod (Deep Fried Bananas)

Boy, am I a sucker for something deep fried! Most especially if it happens to be fruit and so I can kid myself that it's good for me! If there's one thing that Thailand has in abundance, it's bananas, and so it's unsurprising that Thai cuisine offers many a delicious banana-based dish. These little banana bites are the perfect little sweet teaser at the end of a meal. You know, for those times when you need to leave a sweet taste in your palette, but really don't have a whole lot of room left...!

**Makes:** 18

**Preparation time:** 25 minutes + 3 hours sitting

**Ingredients:**

- 6 bananas
- 2 cups rice flour
- 1 egg
- 1 cup coconut milk
- 1 cup fresh coconut meat
- 1 tablespoon sesame seeds
- ¾ cup brown sugar
- Oil for frying

**Serving suggestion:**

If you're looking to make this into more of a 'dish', then try making your own sweet and thick coconut caramel to dip these delightful little bites into! (Recipe is in tips for you!)

1) Set a pan over a low heat.

2) Grate the coconut meat into the pan and mix in the sugar. Let the mixture sit on the heat for about 15 minutes.

3) Then, mix the coconut in a bowl, along with the rice flour, coconut milk, sesame seeds and egg. Let the batter sit for 3 hours.

4) Peel the bananas and chop them into thirds.

5) When the batter has finished sitting, heat roughly 5 cups of oil in a deep saucepan.

6) Dip the banana pieces into the batter to thoroughly coat them, and fry for 2-3 minutes, until the batter has turned golden brown.

7) Place the banana on a paper towel to drain the excess oil before serving.

**Tips:** To make a coconut caramel dipping sauce, try this; in a pan over a medium heat, stir together ¾ of a cup of butter, 1 ½ cups of brown sugar, a good pinch of salt and 2 tablespoons of water. Bring the mixture to the boil and allow it to bubble for 5 minutes. Then, remove the caramel from the heat and stir into it ½ a cup of coconut milk, ½ a teaspoon of coconut extra and a teaspoon of vanilla extract. Simples!

For the banana to be able to hold together during the frying, just ripe bananas that are still pretty firm are the best.

# Thong Yip (Egg Yolk Tarts)

Rather delightfully, 'thong' means 'gold' in Thai. And that, in turn, delightfully means that these tarts are make for special occasions and are full of love and deliciousness. What, in my opinion, makes these little tarts extra special is the inclusion of duck eggs. Duck eggs (unless you're a duck owner, I guess!) and somewhat of a rarity, and to me feel like the perfect way to make something feel that little bit more special.

**Makes:** 12+

**Preparation time:** 85 minutes

**Ingredients:**

- 5 duck eggs
- 5 hen eggs
- 3 cups sugar
- 1 ½ cups jasmine flowers

**Serving suggestion:**

Well, since these are named after gold, they really seem to befit a special occasion! Try as a little sweet treat to pass around a party or gathering.

1) Add the jasmine into a large bowl and pour in 3 cups of boiling water. Cover the bowl and let the flowers steep for 30-40 minutes. Then, strain the water into a large saucepan.

2) Add the sugar into the pan with the jasmine water and stir until the sugar dissolves. Bring the mixture to the boil and then lower it to a simmer and leave it to thicken.

3) Separate the yolks from the whites of all of the eggs and whisk the yolks up until stiff.

4) Remove the jasmine syrup from the heat and drop a heaped teaspoonful of yolk at a time into the syrup. Each spoonful should gather itself into a ball.

5) Place the pan back onto a low heat, and once the egg yolks have become golden, scoop them out and shape them into a star or flower shape with 5 points.

6) Place each little tart into a cup or onto a china plate to firm up before serving.

**Tips:** If you see the syrup thickening up whilst the egg yolks are in there, add a little extra water to keep it thinned. Otherwise, the texture of the egg yolks will be too close.

Please don't waste the egg whites! You can easily refrigerate them and use within a few days to make a frittata, or meringues (even though these aren't Thai dishes, obviously).

# Sang Kaya Faktong (Pumpkin Custard)

Now it's true that many Thai dishes are very summery in their flavours and ingredients, and so therefore may not be best made during the Western 'winter' or 'Fall' time. Ahh, but if it's mid-November and you're finding yourself craving something Thai, we have the solution for you! This classic Thai dish is made with pumpkin, of all things! And, it's really, really yummy!

**Serves:** 6+

**Preparation time:** 70 minutes + at least 1 hour refrigeration

**Ingredients:**

- 4 eggs
- 1 pumpkin
- 1 cup coconut milk
- 1 teaspoon cornstarch
- 1 teaspoon vanilla extract
- ½ cup brown sugar
- Pinch of salt

**Serving suggestion:**

Make some sweet Thai-spiced pumpkin seeds to add some crunch to this dish too.

1) Cut out the top of the pumpkin to create a 'lid'. Scrape out the seeds from the inside.

2) Mix the cornstarch with a little coconut milk and set aside.

3) Into a pan, add the sugar and half of the coconut milk. Stir in the vanilla extract too.

4) Add a pinch of salt and stir until the sugar dissolves. Then, remove from the heat.

5) Then, stir in the remaining coconut milk.

6) Beat the eggs and then whisk them into the coconut milk mixture. Then, also stir in the coconut milk and cornstarch that you mixed together earlier.

7) Pour the mixture into the inside of the custard.

8) Place the pumpkin into a steamer and cook for 45 minutes, so that the custard has firmed up and the pumpkin has become tender.

9) Place the pumpkin into the refrigerator for an hour to cool, before cutting into slices and serving.

**Tips:** So, if you're looking to make those pumpkin seeds like we suggested, here's what to do; rinse and pat dry the pumpkin seeds and then toss them in a mix of ground nutmeg, cinnamon, star anise and cardamom. Spread the seeds out on a baking tray and roast in the oven for 15 minutes.

For obvious reasons (the steamer being the reason!), as fun as it is to choose the most giant pumpkin you can, a smaller one may be better!

# Bua Loy Nam Khing (Sesame Dumplings in Ginger Soup)

Adorably, 'bua loy' means 'floating lotus', which is apparently what the sesame dumplings reminded the creator of this dish of. And in this dish, these 'floating lotuses' are in a pond of ginger soup that really packs a punch. This is another of those wonderful desserts for those who don't have a particularly sweet tooth.

**Serves:** 4

**Preparation time:** 25 minutes

**Ingredients:**

- 5 ¼ oz. rice flour
- 3 ½ oz. brown sugar
- 3 inches fresh ginger
- 1 ¾ oz. black sesame seeds

**Serving suggestion:**

This is not at all heavy and so is a lovely fresh way to end a Thai-inspired meal.

1) Process the sesame seeds into a powder.

2) Then, in a pan, heat half of the brown sugar and stir in the sesame seed powder. The sugar should begin to melt, and so you can stir it together with the sesame seed powder to create a paste. Remove from the heat and set to one side.

3) Put the rice flour into a bowl and dribble in cold water, a tiny amount at a time. Knead the flour into a firm dough ball.

4) Then, pinch of pieces of dough, kind of golf ball sized, and then roll them and flatten them so that you have flat circles.

5) Pinch off a little of the sesame paste and stick it in the middle of your dough. Then, roll the dough up and around it and roll the dough back into a ball, with the sesame paste enclosed in the middle.

6) Set a pan of water on to boil, and then drop the dough balls in. They should take about 3 or 4 minutes in the simmering water, and then they will float to the surface when they're ready.

7) When the balls are ready, scoop them out and into cold water, to stop them from cooking any more.

8) Add 6 ¾ fl oz. of water into a pan over a low heat.

9) Thinly slice the ginger and drop it into the pan of water and stir in the remaining brown sugar.

10) After 10 minutes or so, the water should have thickened a little into a syrup. Taste to check the ginger flavour.

11) Then, serve in bowls, placing 3 or 4 sesame balls into a bowl and pouring ginger syrup over the top.

**Tips:** If you're feeling creative, you can infuse other flavours into the ginger syrup too, like spices or fruits.

Remember not to eat the ginger slices! If you feel that you may forget, you can strain the syrup before serving.

# Pang Gi (Coconut Pancakes)

Now this is my kind of thing – sweet, sweet breakfast, baby! Who doesn't love pancakes? The awesome thing is, that the more I cook, and learn about the food of different places and cultures, the more I realise that pancakes are almost universal! And that, my friends, is not a coincidence, because pancakes are what I call 'instant happy' – just try eating one of these without having a huge grin on your face!

**Serves:** 4

**Preparation time:** 20 minutes

**Ingredients:**

- 1 ripe banana
- 1 ½ cups coconut milk
- ½ cup coconut meat
- 1/3 cup brown sugar
- 1/3 cup desiccated coconut
- Pinch of salt
- Oil for frying (why not coconut?)

**Serving suggestion:**

I cannot tell you how to top your pancakes – that's a deeply personal thing! My suggestion for these particular beauties though, would be fresh pineapple chunks, and, my favourite, chocolate chips!

1) In a pan over a medium heat, put the coconut milk and sugar, and stir until the sugar dissolves. Then, remove the pan from the heat.

2) Mash the banana and shred the coconut flesh.

3) Once the mixture has cooled enough to handle, pour it into a bowl. Stir in the banana, coconut flesh, desiccated coconut, rice flour and a pinch of salt. Mix until there are no (or very few!) lumps.

4) Begin hating a little oil in a pan and spoon a few teaspoonfuls of the batter in at a time, spreading them out to make a small pancake.

5) Cook each pancake for 1-2 minutes on each side, until it's golden brown and firm, and then flip it and cook the same on the other side.

6) If you're cooking a lot, then you can stack the pancakes on a plate and keep them warm in the oven until serving.

**Tips:** It's kind of annoying to take more time, I know, but to avoid pancakes sticking together, it's best to just cook one at a time, unless you know you have the skills!

These pancakes are supposed to be pretty small, so even just 2 inches across is a good size.

# Thai Iced Tea

I'm sure you've tried your fair share of iced teas over time, so why should now be the time to switch from your preferred type to the Thai version? Well, because it's sweet, spicy and delicious, that's why! Some of the ingredients may not be easily found in your local area, but for the full impact of this delicious drink, I honestly do believe that it's worth sourcing them somehow – you can try an Asian market, or even online.

**Serves:** 2

**Preparation time:** 10 minutes

**Ingredients:**

- 2 cardamom pods
- tablespoons loose leaf black tea
- 2 teaspoons coconut milk
- 1 piece of star anise
- 1 cinnamon stick
- 1 tablespoon sugar
- 1 tablespoon sweetened condensed milk
- Pinch of ground tamarind
- Fresh mint to garnish
- Ice for serving

**Serving suggestion:**

Keep a jug of this iced tea in the refrigerator to instantly have a sweet and refreshing drink during the hot weather.

1) Into 1 cup of boiling water, place the loose leaf black tea, star anise, cinnamon, cardamom pods and a sprinkle of ground tamarind. Leave it to steep for 5 minutes and then strain the tea.

2) Into the strained water, stir the sugar and sweetened condensed milk.

3) Fill 2 tall glasses with ice and divide the tea evenly between the 2 glasses, leaving a little room at the top.

4) Pour the coconut milk into the 2 glasses and garnish with a sprig of fresh mint.

**Tips:** If you're looking for a dairy-free version, just replace the condensed milk to coconut cream. This will also give such an exotic flavour!

If you know that you don't have a particularly sweet tooth, then you can leave out the sugar.

# Massaman Chicken Curry

Here's another Thai curry for you to add to your repertoire – always a firm favourite – Massaman. Massaman curry, is, of course, bold on flavour (we'd expect nothing less from a Thai dish, would we?), but, as some of you may be delighted to hear, it's pretty mild in the spice department.

**Serves:** 4

**Preparation time:** 60 minutes

## Ingredients:

- 24 oz. diced chicken pieces
- 14 fl oz. coconut milk
- 4 garlic cloves
- 3 bay leaves
- 3 tablespoons fish sauce
- 2 potatoes
- 2 inches fresh ginger
- 2 tablespoons coconut oil
- 1 red chilli
- 1 onion
- 1 red bell pepper
- 1 tomato
- 1 lemongrass stalk
- 1 tablespoon tamarind
- 1 tablespoon brown sugar
- 1 teaspoon turmeric
- 1 teaspoon ground coriander
- 1 teaspoon cumin seeds
- ½ cup chicken stock
- ¼ cup dry roasted cashews

**Serving suggestion:**

This curry does enough to speak for itself, so plain rice is good enough!

1) Add the oil into a pan on a medium heat and allow it to begin heating.

2) Peel and dice the onion and mince the garlic and ginger. Add them into the pan and stir everything around.

3) After 2 minutes or so, when the pan has become fragrant, pour in the chicken stock.

4) Then, mince the white part of the lemongrass and stir it in. Roughly chop the cashews and add them in too.

5) Then, stir in the bay leaves, tamarind, fish sauce, sugar, ground coriander, cumin seeds and turmeric.

6) Bring the pan to a low boil and add in the diced chicken.

7) Peel and dice the potatoes and stir them in, along with the coconut milk. Bring everything up to the boil and then reduce down to a low simmer for 20 minutes.

8) Dice up the red pepper and tomato and stir them through. Leave the curry simmering for another 10 minutes, to ensure that the chicken and potatoes are thoroughly cooked. Enjoy!

**Tips:** Yes, tamarind can be difficult to get hold of, so if you prefer, you can use lime juice in its place.

Remember that, as this is designed to be a mild curry, taste it before serving, and, if need be, stir in more coconut milk to lessen the spice.

# Pa Thong Ko (Thai Doughnuts)

In what place are doughnuts not amazing? Pretty much every food culture has its own take on them. Germany is proud of their 'berliners', Greece offers 'loukoumades' and in India, you can enjoy 'gulab jabun'. Well, I could continue discussing delicious donuts from all around the globe, or, we could have no further ado and get going with making our own Thai donuts – pa thong ko!

**Makes:** 20

**Preparation time:** 35 minutes

## Ingredients:

- 3 cups plain flour
- 1 teaspoon baking powder
- 1 tablespoon vegetable oil + extra for frying
- Pinch of salt
- 1 teaspoon sugar
- ¼ teaspoon baking soda

## Serving suggestion:

Make a Thai inspired coconut and banana dip and enjoy these sweet little treats warm and fresh with it!

1) Stir together the baking powder, baking soda, sugar and a pinch of salt.

2) Add 1 cup of water into the mix and stir well. Then, gently stir the mixture through into the flour too.

3) Stir in the vegetable oil until everything is well combined and then cover the bowl with plastic wrap. Leave the dough to sit for 4 hours.

4) Begin heating oil to a depth of 4 or 5 inches.

5) Meanwhile, lightly flour a surface and roll the dough roughly with your hands into a long sausage.

6) Cut the dough up into 1 inch pieces, and roll each piece into a ball, and then flatten it into a circle.

7) Drop the donuts, just a few at a time, into the oil, and allow them to fry for 2-3 minutes, until they are golden and rise to the surface.

8) Place the Pa Thong Ko on the paper towel to drain the excess oil off before serving.

**Tips:** These traditional donuts are also often made in cross shapes. To do so, cut the dough into 2 inch strips. Then, take 2 pieces, and stick them together, crossing one over the other, by using a little water.

If you have enough of it, why not fry in coconut oil for that little extra Thai-ness!

# Khao Kha Mu (Boiled Pork Leg)

Any fans of pork around? Then this is the dish for you! Using a pork shank, or hock, and a whole load of fantastic Thai ingredients, we can make of Thailand's most acclaimed dishes – Khao Kha Mu.

**Serves:** 4

**Preparation time:** 20 minutes + at least 2 hours cooking time

**Ingredients:**

- 10 Szechuan peppercorns
- 5 garlic cloves
- 5 black peppercorns
- 4 tablespoons sugar
- 3 chillies
- 3 cups vegetable or peanut oil
- 3 tablespoons soy sauce
- 2 cinnamon sticks
- 2 whole star anise
- 1 pork shank
- 1 teaspoon Chinese 5 spice
- ½ cup white vinegar
- ¼ teaspoon ground coriander
- Pinch of salt

**Serving suggestion:**

Boiled rice and bok choy and simple but delicious sides to make this pork into a whole meal.

1) Heat the oil in a large saucepan, and then place the pork shank into it.

2) Fry the pork shank until golden brown on all sides. Take care to be turning it to avoid the frying being uneven. Then, take it out of the oil and place on a paper towel to drain the excess oil.

3) Pound or process together the garlic cloves, Szechuan peppercorns, black peppercorns and coriander, until you have a smooth paste.

4) Place the pork into a large saucepan and cover it with 8 cups of water.

5) Into the saucepan, add in the garlic paste, cinnamon, star anise, soy sauce and a pinch of salt. Leave the pan simmering for 2-3 hours, until your pork is nicely tender.

6) To make the dipping sauce, pound the chillies and mix them with the vinegar and a pinch of salt.

**Tips:** Try to get a front leg, as it contains more meat and less fat than the back legs!

Also, ensure that your meat is 'fresh', meaning that it has not been smoked or cured in any way.

# Khao Soi (Curried Noodle Soup)

Coconut, curry and chicken all in one delicious soup – what could be better? Khao Soi is said to be of Burmese origin, but is now widely eaten in Thailand, especially in the North. It has all the telltale signs of a fantastic Thai dish – I'm talking spice, saltiness, sweetness and, my personal favourite, coconut! Make a big batch and have this soup on the stove top all week, dipping in for a bowl whenever hunger strikes!

**Serves:** 6

**Preparation time:** 65 minutes

**Ingredients:**

**For the curry paste:**

- 8 garlic cloves
- 4 dried chillies
- 2 inches ginger
- 2 shallots
- 1 tablespoon coriander
- 1 tablespoon turmeric
- 1 teaspoon curry powder
- ¼ cup chopped fresh cilantro

**For the soup:**

- 28 oz. coconut milk
- 42 oz. skinless, boneless chicken thighs
- 16 oz. egg noodles
- 3 tablespoons fish sauce
- 2 cups chicken broth
- 2 tablespoons vegetable oil
- 1 red onion

- 1 cup bean sprouts
- 1 tablespoon sugar

**Serving suggestion:**

I am always of the opinion that soup should have some kind of bread accompanying it to soak up all the deliciousness at the end that the spoon can't quite get! Try making Thai roti to do just that job!

1) First things first – make the curry paste! Cover the dried chillies in boiling water and then cover the bowl. Leave them to soak for 25 minutes, or until softened. Drain the chillies but keep the liquid. Puree the soaked chillies up with the garlic, ginger, shallots, fresh cilantro, coriander, turmeric and curry powder, along with 2 tablespoons of the soaking liquid from the chillies. Add more of the chilli water in, if necessary, to make a smooth paste.

2) Heat the vegetable oil in a large pot and add in the curry paste, stirring occasionally until it is fragrant and the colour has darkened.

3) Add in the coconut milk and chicken broth, and then, once the mixture has come to the boil, add in the chicken pieces.

4) Peel and slice up the onion and add it into the mixture too.

5) Reduce the heat down so that the mixture is simmering, and allow the chicken to cook down until tender, for 20 minutes or so.

6) Then, take out the chicken and shred it.

7) Separately, cook the egg noodles according to the package instructions.

8) Add the chicken back into the soup, along with the fish sauce and sugar, and adjust the flavours to taste.

9) Serve with the noodles in the dish first, topped with the soup, and then sprinkled with the bean sprouts and any other garnishes you'll be using.

**Tips:** Other great toppings for the soup include fresh chillies, fresh cilantro, crispy fried onions or lime wedges.

If you or your diners are not quite up to the level of spice, use only half of the paste in the soup. Then, you will have some left for another batch too!

# Mi Krop (Crispy Stir Fry with Sweet and Sour Sauce)

This is one of those dishes that are probably up there among your takeout favourites. But, it's time to try making it for yourself! The preparation and extra time it takes will be worth it for the extra adding flavour that a little bit of love and TLC adds to a dish.

**Serves:** 4

**Preparation time:** 30 minutes

**Ingredients:**

**For the sauce:**

- 4 tablespoons tamarind juice
- 4 tablespoons lime juice
- 4 tablespoons brown sugar
- 3 tablespoons fish sauce
- 2 teaspoons lime zest
- 2 teaspoons tomato paste

**For the stir fry:**

- 6 green onions
- 6 oz. rice noodles
- 4 oz. shrimp
- 4 oz. pork or chicken
- 4 garlic cloves
- 3 cups peanut oil
- 2 eggs
- 1 red chilli
- Pinch of salt

**Serving suggestion:**

Well, I always enjoy my Thai take out with Thai beer, don't you?

1) Heat the peanut oil up to 400F.

2) Break the rice noodles up into pieces and add them into the oil once it's heated. Once they're browned and puffed up, remove them from the oil, preferably with a slotted spoon. Be careful, as they will take literally seconds to cook!

3) In a pan, combine the tamarind juice, lime juice, brown sugar, fish sauce, lime zest and tomato paste. Bring the mixture to the boil, and then reduce it to a simmer until it thickens. Then, remove it from the heat.

4) Add a little oil into a wok. Mince the garlic and chop the green onion and chilli and add them into the wok to begin to stir fry.

5) Then, add in the shrimp and whichever meat you're using until cooked.

6) Stir in the fried rice noodles and the sweet and sour sauce and enjoy whilst hot.

**Tips:** Since the rice noodles cook so quickly, it may be best to cook them in small batches, rather than all at once.

To garnish, use fresh cilantro, chilli, bean sprouts, and even fried tofu!

# Thai Yellow Curry

Yay! Another curry! You just can never get enough of curry, and believe me, I've tried! This is Thai yellow curry is pretty mild, and so is perfect for a family meal with kids. If you're looking to be able to amp up the spice levels eventually, then in fact, this may be a great place to start!

**Serves:** 6

**Preparation time:** 80 minutes

**Ingredients:**

**For the curry paste:**

- 6 inch piece fresh ginger
- 5 dried chillies
- 4 shallots
- 4 full heads of garlic
- 3 tablespoons turmeric
- 3 tablespoons mild curry powder
- 3 tablespoons lemongrass paste
- 2 teaspoons coriander
- ¼ cup fresh cilantro
- Pinch of salt

**For the curry:**

- 16 oz. skinless, boneless chicken
- 14 oz. coconut cream
- 10 small potatoes
- 2 tablespoons brown sugar
- 2 teaspoons fish sauce
- 1 onion
- 1 tablespoon oil
- 1/3 cup yellow curry paste (see recipe above)

**Serving suggestion:**

How could Thai curry be with anything else other than slightly sticky rice?

To make the curry paste:

1) Preheat the oven to 350F.

2) Peel and slice the shallots and ginger. Arrange the slices on a baking tray and drizzle them with a little oil. Cover the tray with foil. Take the papery outside off of the garlic, and chop off the head, and wrap the bulbs in foil too. Place the garlic onto the baking tray too and bake for 15 minutes.

3) Remove the garlic and then raise the temperature to 400F and continue to roast the shallots and garlic for another 25 minutes until soft and fragrant.

4) Meanwhile, have the dried chillies soaking in a bowl of boiling water. After 15 minutes, drain the soaking water.

5) Into a food processor, add the chillies, ginger, turmeric, curry powder, lemongrass paste, coriander, fresh cilantro and a pinch of salt. Add in the shallots and peel the skin from the garlic and add all of the garlic in too. Process into a smooth paste and store in a jar. You can freeze any paste you don't use to make curry again!

**Curry Preparation:**

6) Now, begin heating a little oil in a pan. Peel and slice the onion and add it to the pan to begin to brown and soften.

7) Then, dice the chicken and add it into the pan, along with the curry paste.

8) Slice the potatoes into small chunks and add them to the pan too.

9) After 3-5 minutes, stir in the coconut cream and ½ a cup of water, and stir well to ensure that everything is coated in the paste and coconut.

10) Leave the curry to simmer for 20-30 minutes, until you can tell that the chicken and potatoes are cooked through.

11) Add in small amounts of the brown sugar and fish paste, tasting as you go to get the balance just right. Enjoy!

**Tips:** I love a thick curry sauce, but if you prefer it a little thinner, you can add in a little extra water to take it to your desired consistency.

We've kept the curry paste mild by using only 5 chillies. If you want it spicier, you can add in as many as you like!

# Pla Nueng Manoa (Garlic Lime Fish)

Garlic and lime is just one of those flavour combinations that I start salivating at the very thought of! And this dish really does do those ingredients justice! The chillies are optional, so this is one of those Thai dishes even for those who don't love the spice! Everything is just so fresh and flavoursome – it's perfect for a summer dinner to enjoy outside.

**Serves:** 2

**Preparation time:** 30 minutes

**Ingredients:**

- 8 tablespoons lime juice
- 6 tablespoons fish sauce
- 5 lemongrass stalks
- 2 heads garlic
- 2 tablespoons sugar
- 1 barramundi
- 1 cup fish stock
- 1 cup fresh cilantro
- Chillies to taste (optional)

**Serving suggestion:**

What could it be other than rice? Some steamed greens too, of course, would be a great idea, to round out the meal.

1) Scale and gut the fish, if necessary. Then, make 3 diagonal incisions on two side of the fish.

2) Chop the tops off of the lemongrass and slightly bruise it. Stuff the lemongrass into the incisions.

3) Steam the fish by filling a saucepan up halfway with boiling water and adding in a rack or metal colander. Place the fish into the rack and cover the pan. It should take 8-15 minutes to cook through, depending on the size of your fish.

4) In another pan, begin heating the fish stock up to the boil. Stir in the sugar until dissolved.

5) Mince up the garlic, cilantro and chillies, if using, and stir into the fish stock, as well as the lime juice and fish sauce. Taste and adjust the balance of flavours if needed.

6) Once the fish is cooked, transfer it to a serving dish. Pour the fish stock sauce over the top of it, and garnish with fresh cilantro and lime wedges to serve.

**Tips:** I am aware that the whole fish is a bit of a turn off for some people. You can, of course, use fish fillets. Just take care, because the cooking time for a smaller piece of fish will be less than for the whole fish. Check the fillets after 5 minutes.

If you don't have barramundi, something similar like tilapia or red snapper.

# Roti

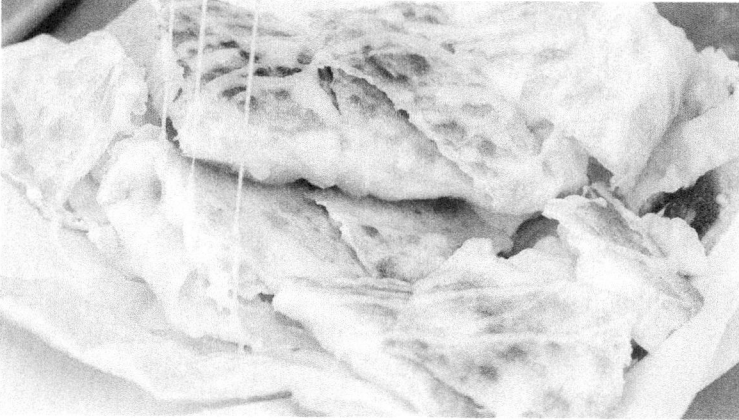

I don't know about you but I love bread! One of the joys of getting to know the cuisine of a new culture, for me, is finding out what kind of bread they have! And boy, was I excited to get to know 'roti'. Similar breads are found in other Asian cuisine, and they're all totally yummy. This roti is the perfect side for almost any Thai dish, especially curries... just imagine mopping up a spicy, fragrant sauce with fresh roti bread made by your own fair hands... let's do this!

**Makes:** 8

**Preparation time:** 45 minutes

**Ingredients:**

- 1 ½ cups plain flour
- 1 tablespoon oil + extra for cooking
- ¾ teaspoon sugar
- ½ teaspoon baking powder
- ¼ cup milk
- Pinch of salt

**Serving suggestion:**

Even if you don't have a curry to serve this with, having some garlic butter melting on this warm fresh bread is a dish from heaven!

1) Mix together the flour, baking powder and a pinch of salt.

2) Warm the milk a little in a saucepan, until you can still touch it, but you can feel the heat!

3) Stir the milk into the flour, along with ¼ cup of warm water and the oil. Bring the ingredients together into a stiff dough.

4) Leave the dough to rest for 30 minutes, and then lightly flour a surface.

5) Divide the dough into 8 equally sized pieces and roll each one out into roughly 6 inch wide disks.

6) Heat the pan and add a small amount of oil or butter in, checking that the pan is evenly coated.

7) Place each roti in onto the heat, and then, when you see it bubbling, flip it over to cook on the other side too. When both sides are golden brown, brush with a little extra butter if you like, and serve.

**Tips:** Make this vegan and even more 'Thai' by using coconut milk in place of the regular milk.

Try to keep the rotis pretty thin so that they'll cook through quickly, before the bread begins to burn or crisp too much.

# Author's Afterthoughts

*Thanks ever so much to each of my cherished readers for investing the time to read this book!*

*I know you could have picked from many other books but you chose this one. So a big thanks for downloading this book and reading all the way to the end.*

*If you enjoyed this book or received value from it, I'd like to ask you for a favor. Please take a few minutes to post an honest and heartfelt review on Amazon.com. Your support does make a difference and helps to benefit other people.*

*Thanks!*

**Daniel Humphreys**

# About the Author

*Daniel Humphreys*

Many people will ask me if I am German or Norman, and my answer is that I am 100% unique! Joking aside, I owe my cooking influence mainly to my mother who was British! I can certainly make a mean Sheppard's pie, but when it comes to preparing Bratwurst sausages and drinking beer with friends, I am also all in!

I am taking you on this culinary journey with me and hope you can appreciate my diversified background. In my 15 years career as a chef, I never had a dish returned to me by one of clients, so that should say something about me! Actually, I will take that back. My worst critic is my four years old son, who refuses to taste anything that is green color. That shall pass, I am sure.

My hope is to help my children discover the joy of cooking and sharing their creations with their loved ones, like I did all my life. When you develop a passion for cooking and my suspicious is that you have one as well, it usually sticks for life. The best advice I can give anyone as a professional chef is invest. Invest your time, your heart in each meal you are creating. Invest also a little money in good cooking hardware and quality ingredients. But most of all enjoy every meal you prepare with YOUR friends and family!

Made in the USA
Coppell, TX
28 October 2020